T0142547

Fearless Felix and His Heroes

Archway Publishing books may be ordered through booksellers or by contacting:

Archway Publishing
1663 Liberty Drive
Bloomington, IN 47403
www.archwaypublishing.com
1 (888) 242-5904

Because of the dynamic nature of the Internet, any web addresses or links contained in this book may have changed since publication and may no longer be valid. The views expressed in this work are solely those of the author and do not necessarily reflect the views of the publisher, and the publisher hereby disclaims any responsibility for them.

Any people depicted in stock imagery provided by Getty Images are models, and such images are being used for illustrative purposes only.
Certain stock imagery © Getty Images.

ISBN: 978-1-4808-7096-3 (sc)
ISBN: 978-1-4808-7097-0 (hc)
ISBN: 978-1-4808-7095-6 (e)

Print information available on the last page.

Archway Publishing rev. date: 10/30/2018

Fearless Felix and His Heroes

David Volk

This book is dedicated to all dogs and the incredible service, joy, and loyalty they have brought to people for centuries.

Acknowledgments

As with all books, this book owes much to other people who helped me tell the story of Felix and the wonderful service and joy that all dogs bring to us.

First, I would like to thank Donna Wiese, who had the idea for this book and made it possible, and her husband, Mitch, who works with Felix and who gave great assistance.

I would like to thank the "Smoky War Dog, LLC" for their help in getting approval for the use of her picture. A special acknowledgment goes to Bill Wynne, who was Smoky's owner and trainer, and is now a ninety-six-year-old veteran. Thanks for your service, Bill."

I wish to thank the National Archives and the American History Museum at the Smithsonian. Both were extremely helpful in securing the images of two war dogs, Stubby from World War I and Chips from World War II.

Thanks to my friend Becky Carmody and her nine-year-old granddaughter Ila, who gave me the benefit of their thoughts and edits. Finally, appreciation to brother Craig, who has been of immense help with all six of my previous books.

Hi, kids. My name is Felix, and I am a three-year-old German shepherd. I have a story I want to tell you. It's a story about my job and that of other dogs like me. First, however, I want to tell you about myself.

Here I am in the beautiful Black Hills of South Dakota.

As I mentioned, my name is Felix, but the name on my birth certificate is Felix Von Iron Cross. Doesn't that sound impressive? It's much too long and formal for me, so I'm just Felix.

I live in Sioux Falls, South Dakota, with my mom and dad and my little brother and sister. Of course they aren't my real mom and dad or brother or sister, but we are so close and love each other so much that they will always feel like my real family.

My mom's name is Donna, and my dad is Mitch. Mom simply spoils me, but I work with Dad. I will tell you more about the work I do later in my story. My brother's name is Cody, and he is a wheaten terrier.

My sister is Miss Kitty, and she is a dachshund. I told you they were my little brother and sister, but they are both older than I am. They seem little because I'm the biggest! Woof!

When I first met them, they barked at me a lot. At first I thought they didn't like me, but it was just because I was new, strange, and big to them. We have become great friends as time has passed.

Most of the time I am just a normal dog who loves playing. My best friend is the neighbor's dog, Sammy. When we are both in our back-yards, we run back and forth along our fence and bark. It's not angry barking or warning barking—we're just so very glad to see each other. Anyway, it is great to have a best friend, and I hope you all have a good friend too.

I am getting ready to play with Sammy. Like all
little brothers, Cody also wants to play.

In addition to playing with Cody, Kitty, and Sammy, I like to watch
television. I especially like old Rin Tin Tin reruns. He was a hero and
a very smart dog. I like other animal shows on Animal Planet, but I
think I like Rin Tin Tin the best because he is a German shepherd
like I am.

As I mentioned, most of the time I am just another playful, happy dog.
However, I also have an important job. That job is to keep people safe!
You see, I am a dog who sniffs out danger. I was trained for more than
sixteen months to be able to sniff out the different chemicals used to
make bombs, and I then spent six weeks training with my dad, Mitch,
to work as a team.

While all of us have special skills and talents, one thing we dogs do very well is smell. Our sense of smell is forty times stronger than people's. You kids can identify more than a million different scents, while we can identify more than 250 million. That is why we are so good at detecting things that might be used in making a bomb.

So when there are going to be large crowds or a lot of people in one place, my dad and I go to work. I go through the building or arena and smell to see if there is anything that might be dangerous. When Mitch and I are walking through a building and I detect something, all I do is sit down. I don't bark or jump around—I just sit near where I smell something that might be bad.

What is my reward for doing this work? Mitch has a blue rubber ball that I just love, and that is how I get paid. I know you are thinking that isn't much of a reward and that I should get a better treat than that, but that ball is super important to me. Also, Mom gives me a lot of treats.

Another interesting thing about working with Dad is that he gives me commands in a foreign language. You see, if we are working where there are people, we don't want someone saying something simple like "sit" and confusing me. Also, even though I love to be petted and hugged, Mitch doesn't allow that while I am working as that also distracts me. In fact, Dad even puts a sign on me that says "Do Not Pet" when we are working.

I was in training for many months, which was hard, but Mitch and I got along wonderfully right from the start. In addition to training, Mitch and I also put on exhibits to show people how I find and identify dangerous things. I especially like to go to schools and be with kids like you. You're my favorites, and you always treat me so nicely.

Another neat part of my job is that we get to travel. We go to car races and big concerts all over the country.

Here I am on the plane. Dad's asleep next to me but I'm too excited

When we are at these events, I get to meet bomb dogs from everywhere. It's nice to meet these new friends, but when it's time to search for danger, we're all business.

However, it isn't all work and training, and most of the time I lead a fun, normal dog's life.

I know you kids all have heroes that you watch on TV and in the movies, characters like Superman, Batman, Spiderman, Black Panther, and others. Not me. Rin Tin Tin, remember? Now, though, I would like to tell you about some heroes who were real dogs and did incredible things.

We dogs have been serving our country for many, many years, and some of our stories are truly amazing. These dogs I call warrior dogs.

Sergeant Stubby was an American pit bull terrier, and he served with an army unit a long time ago during World War I. It was 1917, more than one hundred years ago, and Stubby saw action in seventeen battles with his friends and fellow soldiers in the 102nd Infantry. He would warn soldiers of incoming poisonous gas attacks and artillery and locate wounded soldiers who were hard to find. Sergeant Stubby was the first dog to be given a rank in the army.

Chips, a collie-German shepherd-husky mix, served in World War II, and he was the most decorated dog of that war. He was awarded the Distinguished Service Cross, Purple Heart (you get this medal when you are wounded), and the Silver Star. Perhaps his most famous exploit was his assault on a machine gun position where he took ten enemy soldiers prisoner.

There are many more stories of dogs and their heroism and bravery in helping to keep people safe. Smoky also served in World War II and was in dozens of combat missions and more than 150 air raids in the Pacific. Smoky was a Yorkshire terrier. She was small, but she used her size to her advantage as she once pulled a telegraph wire through a narrow seventy-foot pipe. This saved time and possibly the lives of the engineers who would have been exposed to enemy fire.

Photo courtesy Smoky War Dog, LLC

As I said, there are many stories of dogs doing heroic things for the people they served, and I will tell you just one more of those stories.

Nemo was a German shepherd also. He fought in the Vietnam War, and after his handler was wounded and fell unconscious, Nemo crawled on top of him to protect him from further injury even though he was also wounded.

These are just a few stories of heroic dogs that served our country, and they truly are my heroes. I am proud to walk in their pawprints as I work to keep people safe.

There are also many working dogs that don't sniff out danger or go into battle. They come in all shapes and sizes and are called service dogs. They perform many duties that make people's lives better.

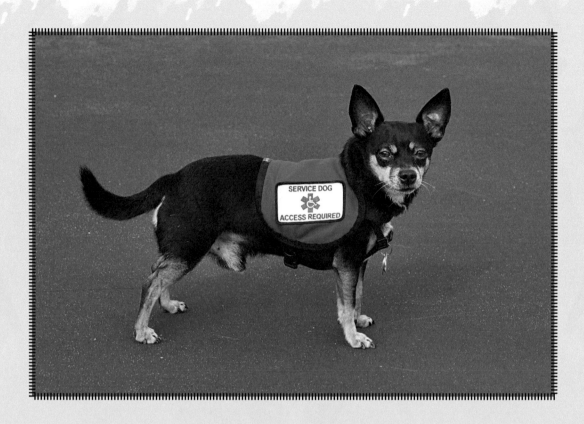

Perhaps the working dog we are most familiar with and that has been around the longest is the guide dog. These dogs are trained to help people who have problems seeing (who are partially or completely blind). Guide dogs have been around for centuries, maybe all the way back to ancient Rome more than two thousand years ago!

However, guide dogs are just one kind of working dog that provide assistance to humans. There are hearing dogs that can warn people of noises such as alarms, doorbells, or crying babies.

There are mobility-assistance dogs that help people who are disabled, and they perform many duties for them. They can get a phone when it rings or get something from the refrigerator and bring it to their owner.

There are also seizure-alert dogs that warn when their humans might be about to have a seizure and allergy-detection dogs that can warn their people to avoid those things that they are allergic to and that could cause them harm. They even have small dogs that can smell out pesky bedbugs and termites. I am proud of all of these working dogs that provide such great service to people who have problems in their lives.

Finally, scientists are now studying whether dogs can smell a disease before those diseases can be detected by medical science. This is especially important with the horrible disease of cancer because the sooner you detect cancer, the sooner you can treat it, and chances of curing it get much better.

Dogs serve people in many helpful ways and have for hundreds of years. We love our work because we love people, and keeping people safe is one way we can show that love.

Kids, I hope you have enjoyed my story about working dogs and the service we have provided in the past and continue to provide today. But now it's time for me to be just a normal dog. I hear Sammy barking in the backyard, which means it's time for us to chase each other along the fence. Also, I'm going to try to catch bugs that are flying. It isn't easy to catch a fast-moving bug, but every once in a while I get lucky. Either way, it's great fun.

Finally, I just want to tell you that even though I've been trained to find explosives, I hope I never do. I just want everyone to be safe, so I will continue to do my job.

Woof, woof!

A Message from Felix's Mom, Donna

Dear readers,

When we first got Felix, I had trouble separating his identity as a working bomb dog from his identity as a pet. However, very quickly my husband, Mitch, and I realized how special this wonderful dog is and how important he is to our family. Then I discovered that the owner of our local bakery was named Mitch and that he had a young son named Felix who had been battling cancer and who loves German shepherds. So I wanted to celebrate this incredible coincidence and tell the story of our Felix and other dogs that bring so much to our lives and do so much to make our lives better. I want to honor that young man, Felix, and young people everywhere who are fighting the horrible disease of cancer. I hope you enjoy this book, and I hope it will motivate you to go and rescue a dog that is in need of a good home.

Donna Marie Wiese

AUTHOR

David Volk was born and raised in Mitchell, South Dakota. In 1969, after graduating from college, he was drafted into the United States Army. He served two years in the army, one of which was in Vietnam. He served as a combat photographer with the 101st Airborne Division and was awarded the Army Commendation Medal and Bronze Star while in Vietnam.

In 1972, at the age of twenty-five, he was elected state treasurer of South Dakota, the youngest person in the state's history elected to statewide office. He was reelected four times.

Volk has published six books, including *Draftee: A High School Teacher Goes to War*, which chronicles his time in the army, and *My Grandpa's War*, a children's book about Vietnam. He has also coauthored four books with Mark Meierhenry: *Mystery of the Round Rocks*, *Mystery of the Tree Rings*, *Mystery of the Maize*, and *Mystery of Pheasants*. Two of these books were selected by Independent Publisher as outstanding regional children's books.

Printed in the United States
By Bookmasters